Lions
Up Close

Carmen Bredeson

Enslow Elementary

CONTENTS

WORDS TO KNOW

canine (KAY nyn)—One of the pointed teeth that animals use to tear off food.

herds (HURDZ)—Groups of animals that live together.

prey (PRAY)—An animal that is food for another animal.

tuft (TUFT)—A bunch of hair held together at one end.

Parts of a Lion

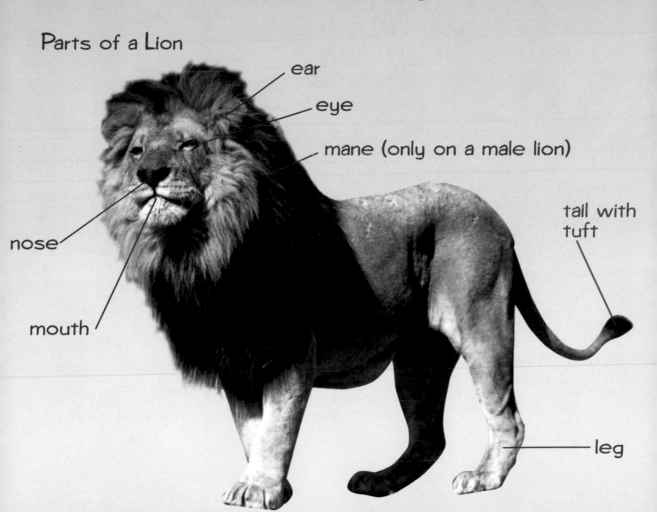

ear

eye

mane (only on a male lion)

tail with tuft

nose

mouth

leg

LION HOMES

Most lions live in the grasslands of Africa.
Herds of grass-eating animals also live there.
The lions have many animals to hunt.

A female lion is
called a lioness.

Most lions live in the part of Africa that is colored purple.

Lions sleep a lot. Some climb trees to take a nap.

LION HAIR

Lions like to hide in tall grass. Their light brown hair is the same color as the grass. A male lion has long, thick hair around his head and neck. This hair is called a mane.

LION EYES

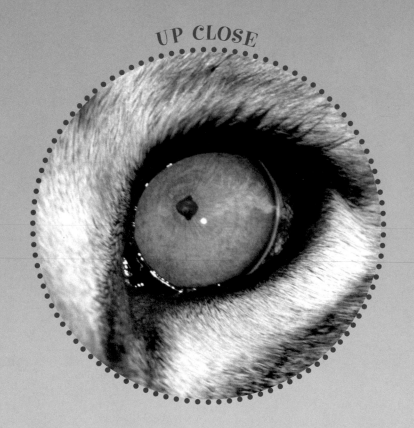

A lion has big gold eyes. They look for **prey** to eat. Lions usually hunt for food at night. They can see much better in the dark than we can. Their eyes glow in the dark when light shines on them.

LION NOSE

A lion can smell very well with its big nose. Smelling helps a lion find food. Lions hunt animals like zebras, giraffes, and wild pigs. They also steal meat that other animals are eating.

LION EARS

A lion can turn its ears many ways.
This helps the lion find animals to eat.
The lion listens. Is the prey behind or
in front? Lions can hear animals that
are very far away.

LION PAWS

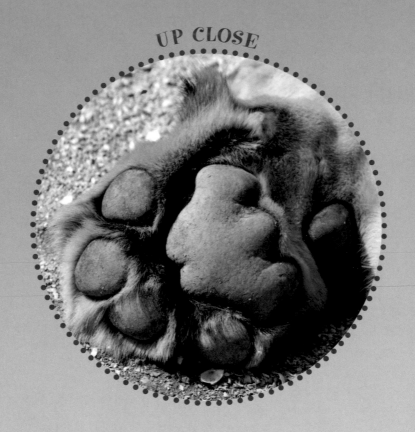

Lion paws have soft pads on the bottom.
A lion can walk very quietly. There are five claws
on each front paw. There are four claws on each
back paw. A lion grabs its prey with its sharp claws.

LION MOUTH

A lion has four **canine** teeth. These long teeth bite the prey. Other teeth cut through the skin and tear meat from the bones. Lions do not chew. They tear off pieces of meat and swallow them whole.

LION TAIL

A lion has a long tail. There is a **tuft** of black hair at the end of the tail. Mother lion swishes her tail back and forth. Lion cubs chase the black tuft like kittens playing with string.

LION CUBS

This lion cub is three days old.

Lion cubs are tiny and blind when they are born. Their mother keeps them hidden in the tall grass for a few weeks. Other animals might try to kill the cubs. When the cubs are bigger, they play games with each other.

LIFE CYCLE

Newborn lion cubs weigh only three pounds.

Young cubs learn to hunt.

Adult lions can live for fifteen years.

LEARN MORE

BOOKS

Anderson, Jill. *Wild Ones: Lions*. Minnetonka, Minn.: Northword Press, 2006.

Squire, Ann. *Lions*. New York: Scholastic, 2005.

Stefoff, Rebecca. *Lions*. New York: Benchmark Books, 2006.

WEB SITES

Creature Feature: Lions
<http://www.nationalgeographic.com/kids/creature_feature/0109/>

San Diego Zoo's Animal Profiles for Kids: Lions of Lion Camp
<http://www.sandiegozoo.org/kids/animal_lions.html>

INDEX

Series Literacy Consultant:
Allan A. De Fina, Ph.D.
Past President of the New Jersey Reading Association
Chairperson, Department of Literacy Education
New Jersey City University
Jersey City, New Jersey

Science Consultant:
Patrick Thomas, Ph.D.
General Curator
Bronx Zoo
Wildlife Conservation Society
Bronx, New York

Note to Parents and Teachers: The **Zoom In on Animals!** series supports the National Science Education Standards for K–4 science. The Words to Know section introduces subject-specific vocabulary words, including pronunciation and definitions. Early readers may need help with these new words.

Enslow Elementary, an imprint of Enslow Publishers, Inc.

Enslow Elementary® is a registered trademark of Enslow Publishers, Inc.

Copyright © 2008 by Carmen Bredeson

Library of Congress Cataloging-in-Publication Data

Bredeson, Carmen.
Lions up close / Carmen Bredeson.
p. cm. — (Zoom in on animals)
Summary: 'This book provides an up-close look at lions for new readers'—Provided by publisher.
Includes index.
ISBN-13: 978-0-7660-3080-0
ISBN-10: 0-7660-3080-6
1. Lions—Juvenile literature. I. Title.
QL737.C23B73 2008
599.757—dc22   2007025610

Printed in the United States of America

10 9 8 7 6 5 4 3 2 1

Photo Credits: © Adam Jones/Visuals Unlimited, pp. 1, 22 (bottom); © Anup Shah/naturepl.com, pp. 15, 17; Art Wolfe/Photo Researchers Inc., p. 21; © Arthur Morris/Visuals Unlimited, p. 18; Artville, p. 5 (map); Charles V. Angelo/Photo Researchers, Inc., pp. 20, 22 (top left); © Digital Vision/Punchstock, p. 19; Eric Gaba, p. 5 (shading on map); © Fritz Polking/Visuals Unlimited, p. 22 (top right); © Hamman/Heldring/Animals Animals, p. 7; © Joanna Van Gruisen/ardea.com, p. 9; © 2007 Jupiterimages Corporation, p. 3; Millard H. Sharp/Photo Researchers Inc., p. 6; © NHPA/Martin Harvey, p. 13; Nigel J. Dennis/Photo Researchers, Inc., pp. 4–5; © Richard DuToit/naturepl.com, p. 8; Shutterstock, pp. 10, 12, 14, 16; © Thomas Dressler/ardea.com, p. 11.

Front Cover Photos: © Adam Jones/Visuals Unlimited (left); © Richard DuToit/naturepl.com (center right); Shutterstock (top right, bottom right).

Back Cover Photo: © 2007 Jupiterimages Corporation.

Enslow Elementary
an imprint of
Enslow Publishers, Inc.
40 Industrial Road
Box 398
Berkeley Heights, NJ 07922
USA
http://www.enslow.com